Will Todd
Passion Music

for female gospel soloist,
SATB, and jazz ensemble

MUSIC DEPARTMENT

OXFORD
UNIVERSITY PRESS

OXFORD
UNIVERSITY PRESS

Great Clarendon Street, Oxford OX2 6DP,
United Kingdom

Oxford University Press is a department of the University of Oxford.
It furthers the University's aim of excellence in research, scholarship,
and education by publishing worldwide. Oxford is a registered trade mark of
Oxford University Press in the UK and in certain other countries

First published 2018

ISBN 978-0-19-352380-7

Music and text origination by
Andrew Jones

Printed in Great Britain on acid-free paper by
Halstan & Co. Ltd, Amersham, Bucks.

Contents

Composer's note

Since composing *Mass in Blue* in 2003 I have been searching for another large-scale project in which to showcase my love of jazz improvising and the beauty and energy of the choral sound. Finally, in 2017, an opportunity arose to create a new jazz choral work for the choirs of St Martin-in-the-Fields, and *Passion Music* is the product of that. The work is an exploration of Easter-themed texts, roughly following the contours of the passion narrative, and uses a soloist as an inspirational and evangelistic voice leading the emotional direction of the complete piece, rather than in the traditional sense of narrating the gospel text. I was thrilled to be able to work with Shaneeka Simon in developing a truly gospel solo part to weave in and around the ensemble and choral textures.

Passion Music has nine movements, mixing hymn texts, gospel quotations, and texts of my own. The rhythm section music, although fully notated, will benefit from improvising performers, who are encouraged to bring their own ideas and textures to the work, making use of the chord symbols. It is also expected that the solo part will be embellished in performance, and there are free improvising sections indicated by wavy lines and appropriate chord symbols. Not all the notated ornamentation needs to be followed—the soloist should feel free to find their own authentic gospel style. Note that the keyboard reduction in the vocal score is for rehearsal only, and the full ensemble backing is required for performance. Pedalling in the keyboard part is marked when specific effects are required; otherwise the player should use the pedal *ad lib.* throughout. *Passion Music* may also be performed liturgically with interspersed readings.

Duration: *c.*40 mins

This note may be reproduced as required for programme notes.

Passion Music was first performed by the choirs of St Martin-in-the-Fields and The Will Todd Ensemble, with Shaneeka Simon, directed by the composer, on 27 March 2018 at St Martin-in-the-Fields, London.

Texts and translations

These texts may be reproduced as required for programme notes.

1. Greater Love

John 15: 13

Greater love has no man, no greater love than this, than to lay down his life for his friends.

2. We Believe

Mrs Cecil Frances Alexander (1818–95)

There is a green hill far away,
Without a city wall,
Where the dear Lord was crucified,
Who died to save us all.

We may not know, we cannot tell,
What pains he had to bear,
But we believe it was for us
He hung and suffered there.

He died that we might be forgiven,
He died to make us good,
That we might go at last to heaven,
Saved by his precious blood.

There was no other good enough
To pay the price of sin;
For only he could unlock the gate
Of heaven and let us in.

3. A New Commandment

John 13: 34

I give you a new commandment:
That you love one another as I have loved you.

4. Love Unknown

Samuel Crossman (1624–84)

My song is love unknown,
My saviour's love to me;
Love to the loveless shown,
That they might lovely be.
O who am I, that for my sake
My Lord should take frail flesh and die?

Contents

Composer's note

Since composing *Mass in Blue* in 2003 I have been searching for another large-scale project in which to showcase my love of jazz improvising and the beauty and energy of the choral sound. Finally, in 2017, an opportunity arose to create a new jazz choral work for the choirs of St Martin-in-the-Fields, and *Passion Music* is the product of that. The work is an exploration of Easter-themed texts, roughly following the contours of the passion narrative, and uses a soloist as an inspirational and evangelistic voice leading the emotional direction of the complete piece, rather than in the traditional sense of narrating the gospel text. I was thrilled to be able to work with Shaneeka Simon in developing a truly gospel solo part to weave in and around the ensemble and choral textures.

Passion Music has nine movements, mixing hymn texts, gospel quotations, and texts of my own. The rhythm section music, although fully notated, will benefit from improvising performers, who are encouraged to bring their own ideas and textures to the work, making use of the chord symbols. It is also expected that the solo part will be embellished in performance, and there are free improvising sections indicated by wavy lines and appropriate chord symbols. Not all the notated ornamentation needs to be followed—the soloist should feel free to find their own authentic gospel style. Note that the keyboard reduction in the vocal score is for rehearsal only, and the full ensemble backing is required for performance. Pedalling in the keyboard part is marked when specific effects are required; otherwise the player should use the pedal *ad lib.* throughout. *Passion Music* may also be performed liturgically with interspersed readings.

Duration: *c.*40 mins

This note may be reproduced as required for programme notes.

Passion Music was first performed by the choirs of St Martin-in-the-Fields and The Will Todd Ensemble, with Shaneeka Simon, directed by the composer, on 27 March 2018 at St Martin-in-the-Fields, London.

Texts and translations

These texts may be reproduced as required for programme notes.

1. Greater Love

John 15: 13

Greater love has no man, no greater love than this, than to lay down his life for his friends.

2. We Believe

Mrs Cecil Frances Alexander (1818–95)

There is a green hill far away,
Without a city wall,
Where the dear Lord was crucified,
Who died to save us all.

We may not know, we cannot tell,
What pains he had to bear,
But we believe it was for us
He hung and suffered there.

He died that we might be forgiven,
He died to make us good,
That we might go at last to heaven,
Saved by his precious blood.

There was no other good enough
To pay the price of sin;
For only he could unlock the gate
Of heaven and let us in.

3. A New Commandment

John 13: 34

I give you a new commandment:
That you love one another as I have loved you.

4. Love Unknown

Samuel Crossman (1624–84)

My song is love unknown,
My saviour's love to me;
Love to the loveless shown,
That they might lovely be.
O who am I, that for my sake
My Lord should take frail flesh and die?

He came from his blest throne,
Salvation to bestow;
But men made strange,
And none the longed-for Christ would know.
But O, my friend, my friend indeed,
Who at my need his life did spend.

Sometimes they strew his way
And his sweet praises sing;
Resounding all the day
Hosannas to their King.
Then 'crucify!' is all their breath,
And for his death they thirst and cry.

Why, what hath my Lord done?
What makes this rage and spite?
He made the lame to run,
He gave the blind their sight.
Sweet injuries! Yet they at these
Themselves displease, and 'gainst him rise.

Here might I stay and sing,
No story so divine;
Never was love, dear King,
Never was grief like thine.
This is my friend, in whose sweet praise
I all my days could gladly spend.

5. Stabat Mater

13th-cent. Latin hymn, trans. Edward Caswall (1814–78)

Stabat Mater dolorosa
Juxta crucem lacrimosa
Dum pendebat Filius.
Stabat Mater lacrimosa.

At the Cross her station keeping,
stood the mournful Mother weeping,
close to her Son to the last.

O quam tristis et afflicta
Fuit illa benedicta
Mater Unigeniti.
Stabat Mater lacrimosa.

O how sad and sore distressed
was that Mother, highly blest,
of the sole-begotten One.

Quis non posset contristari
Christi Matrem contemplari
Dolentem cum Filio?
Stabat Mater lacrimosa.

Can the human heart refrain
from partaking in her pain,
in that Mother's pain untold?

6. The Seven Last Words from the Cross

Will Todd, quoting The Holy Bible

Before the thunder clap, before the sky went black,
Before the temple curtain was rent in two,
Before he breathed his last, before he bowed his head,
Listen to the words that my saviour said.

Before he gave his life, he spoke these words,
Spoke Seven Last Words from the cross.

And as he hung in shame between the worst of men,
As he felt the pain and felt the agony;
Before the earth heaved up and the moon went red,
Listen to the words that my saviour said.

Before he gave his life, he spoke these words,
Spoke Seven Last Words from the cross:

'Father, forgive them, for they know not what they do.'
'Today you will be with me in paradise.'

And as he hung there, he saw his mother's face,
Looked in her eyes and saw the love and grace.
A disciple stood at her side.
Listen to the words that my saviour cried:

'Behold your son, behold your mother.'
That's what he cried from the cross.

He cried in agony, O how he cried to me,
He cried aloud as he hung on the tree.
He was bent in pain and he was close to dead.
Listen to the words that my saviour said:

'My God, why have you forsaken me on the cross?'
He said: 'I thirst.'
'It is finished.'
'Into your hands, Father, I commit my spirit.'
That's how he died on the cross.

Hear the precious words that my saviour said,
Before the sky went black.

7. My Love has Died for Me

Will Todd

My Lord is gone away,
My Lord is gone away,
My Lord is gone away and I have no place to go.

My friend is lost to me,
My friend is lost to me,
My friend is lost to me and I have no place to go.

The fire that leapt so brightly
Burned into eternity,
Heaven taken from me.

My love has died for me,
My love has died for me,
My love has died for me. I have no place to go.

8. Do not stand at my grave and weep

Mary Elizabeth Frye (1905–2004)

Do not stand at my grave and weep;
I am not there. I do not sleep.

I am a thousand winds that blow.
I am the diamond glints on snow.
I am the sunlight on ripened grain.
I am the gentle autumn rain.

When you awaken in the morning's hush,
I am the swift uplifting rush
Of quiet birds in circled flight.
I am the soft stars that shine at night.

Do not stand at my grave and cry;
I am not there. I did not die.
Do not stand at my grave and weep.

9. Were you there?

American Spiritual text

Were you there when they crucified my Lord?
Sometimes it causes me to tremble, tremble;
Were you there when they crucified my Lord?

Were you there when they laid him in the tomb?
Sometimes it causes me to tremble, tremble;
Were you there when they laid him in the tomb?

Were you there when they nailed him to the tree?
Sometimes it causes me to tremble, tremble;
Were you there when they nailed him to the tree?

Were you there when he rose out of the tomb?

We believe it was for us he rose from the dead.
He died for us and he rose for us.
He died to save us.

(reprise from Movement 1)

Greater love has no man than this, no greater love than this, than to lay down his life for his friends.
There is no greater love than this.

Also available:

Passion Music score and set of parts (pno, bass, drum kit, sax (sop/alto), tpt, tbn, timp/perc)
(ISBN 978-0-19-352565-8)

A complete backing track and individual rehearsal tracks for the vocal parts are also available to download from www.oup.com/passionmusic.

Passion Music

Commissioned for the choirs of St Martin-in-the-Fields, London

Passion Music

WILL TODD

1. *Greater Love*

John 15: 13

Printed in Great Britain

OXFORD UNIVERSITY PRESS, MUSIC DEPARTMENT, GREAT CLARENDON STREET, OXFORD OX2 6DP

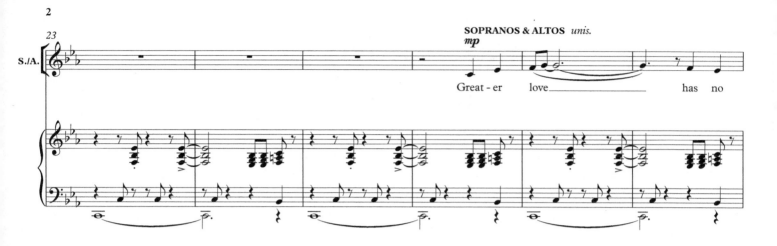

SOPRANOS & ALTOS *unis.*

Great - er love _____ has no

man, ___ no great - er love _____ than this, _____

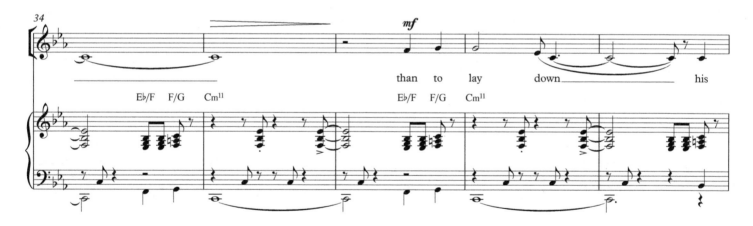

than to lay down _____ his

life _____ for_ his friends. _____

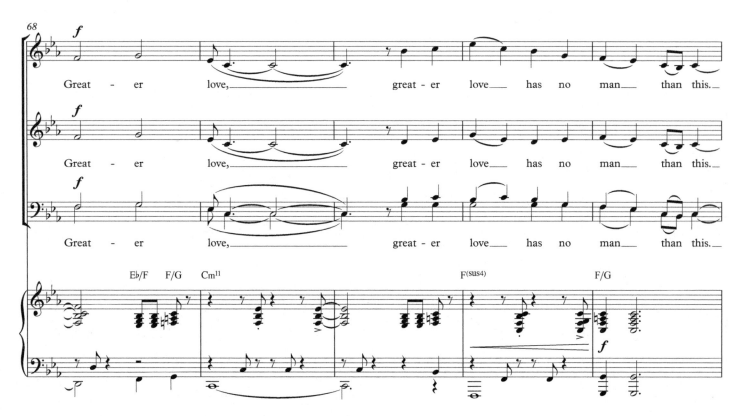

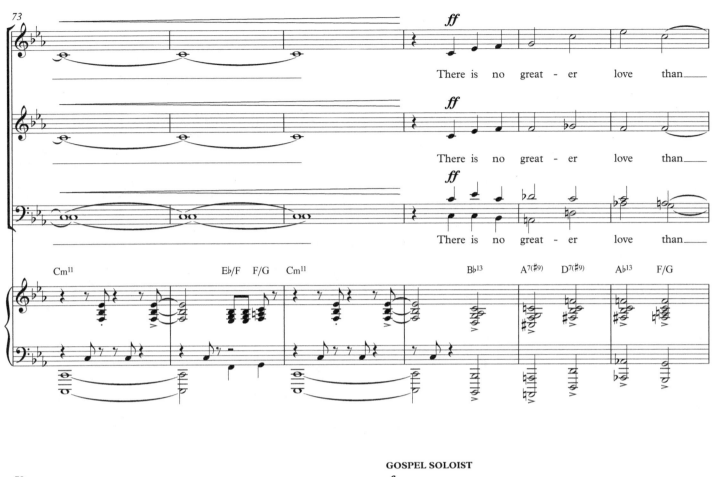

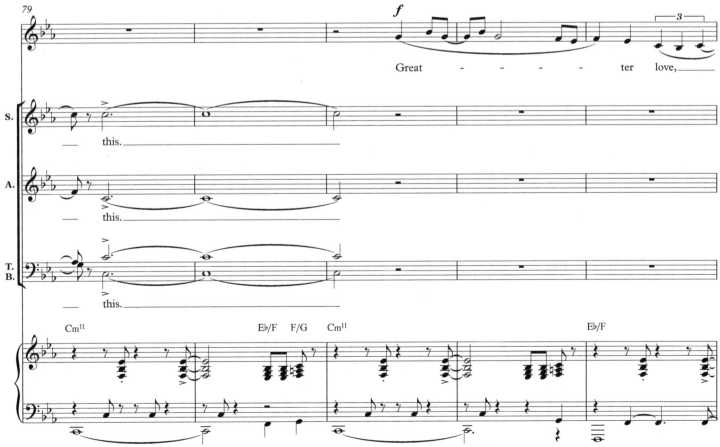

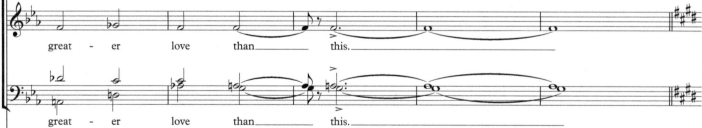

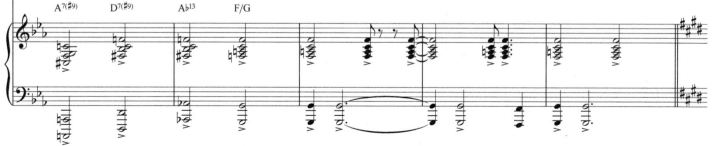

2. We Believe

Mrs Cecil Frances Alexander (1818–95)

14

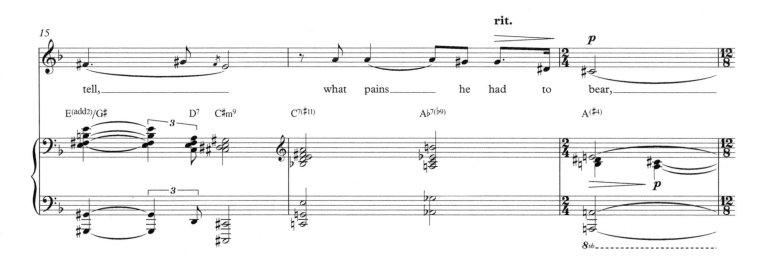

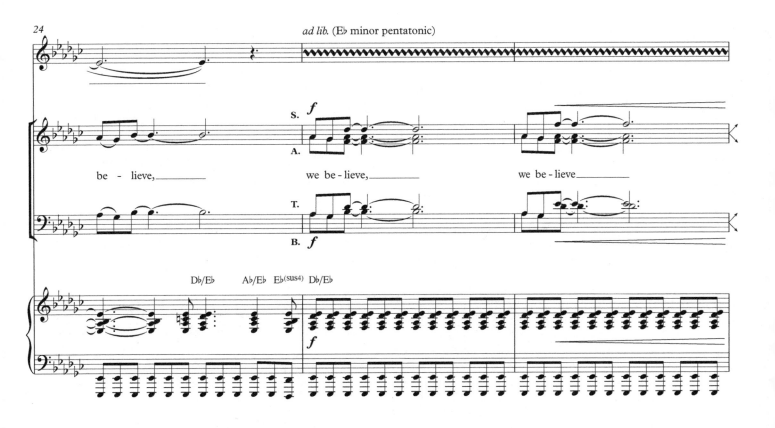

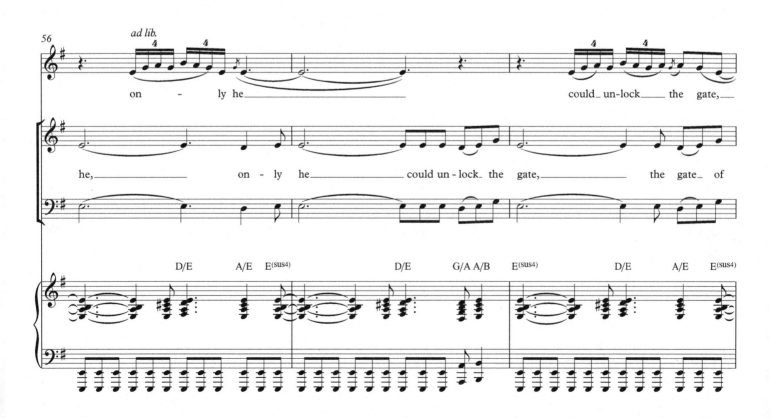

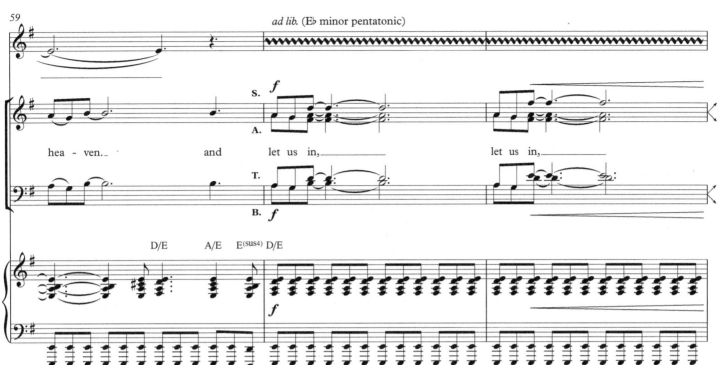

22

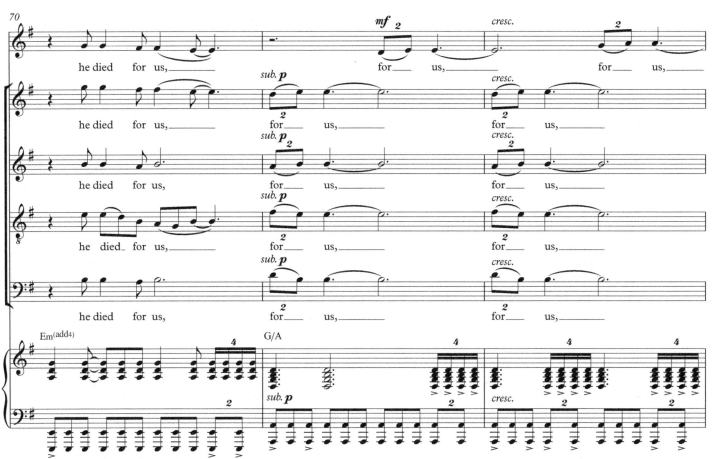

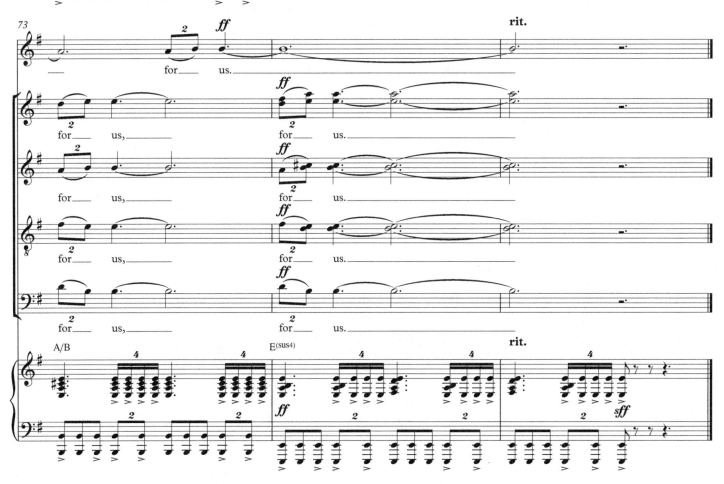

24

3. *A New Commandment*

John 13: 34

26

30

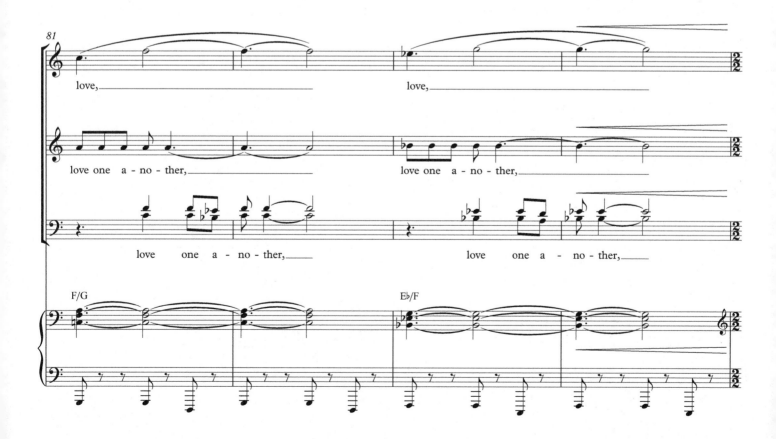

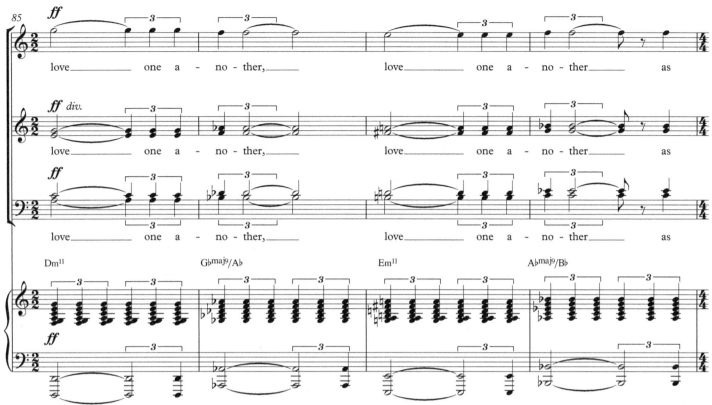

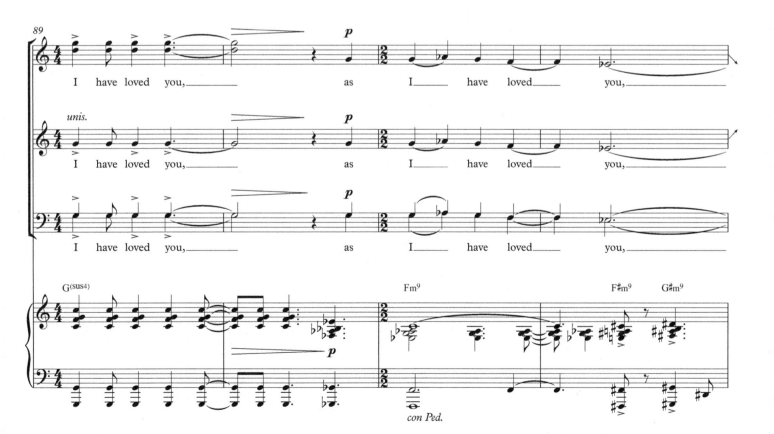

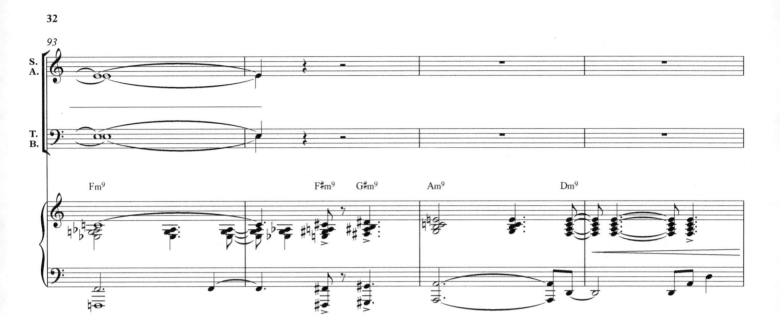

as I_____ have_____ loved you._____

That you love,___ that you love,___

33

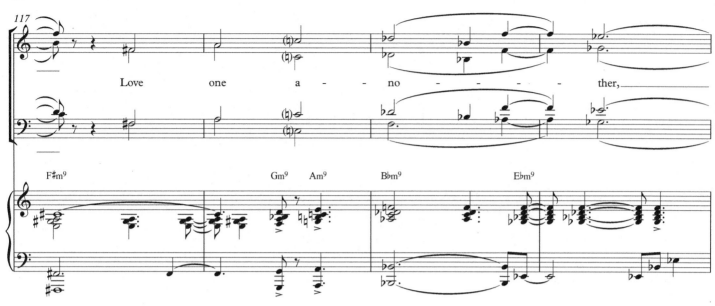

Love one a - no - - - ther,_____

_____ love_____ one a - no - ther, love one a - no - ther,_

love one a - no - ther, love one a - no - ther._____ love one a - no - ther, love one a - no - ther,_

36

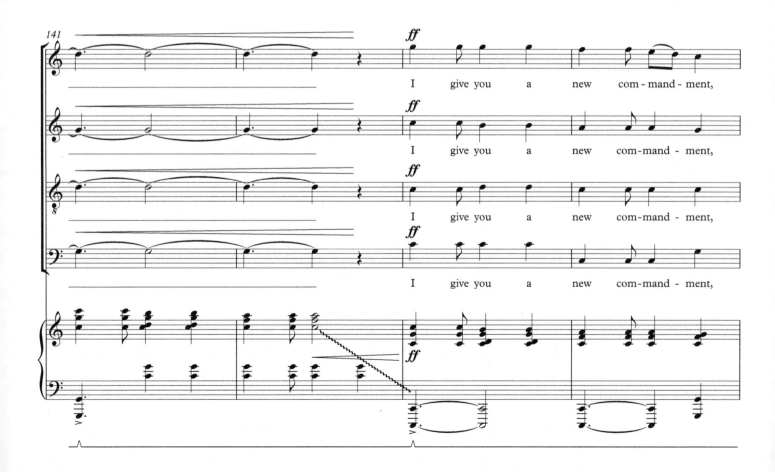

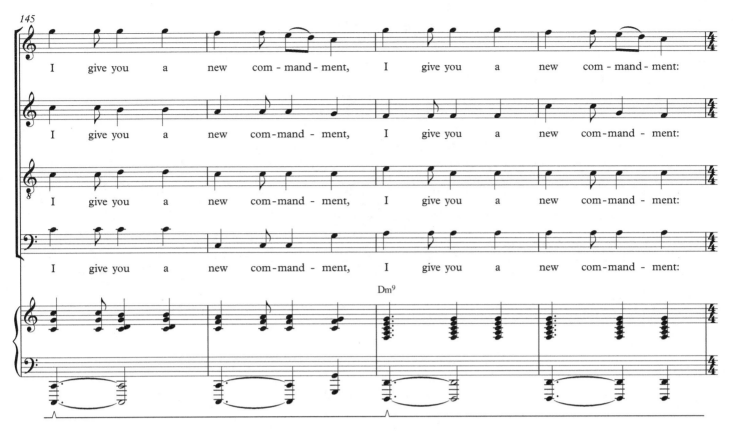

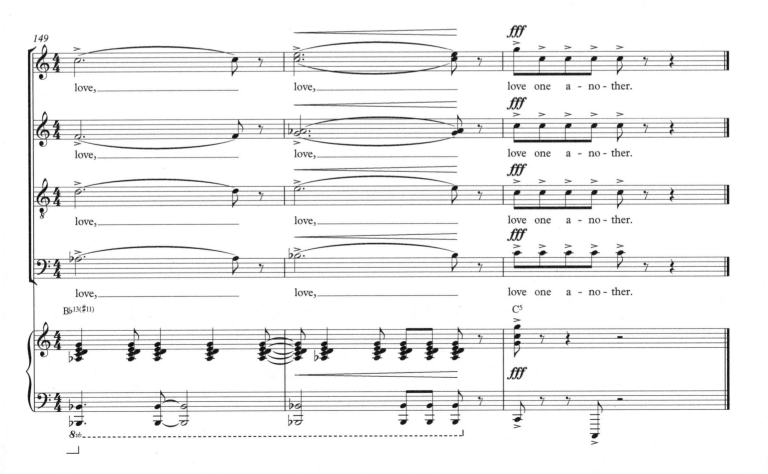

4. *Love Unknown*

Samuel Crossman (1624–84)

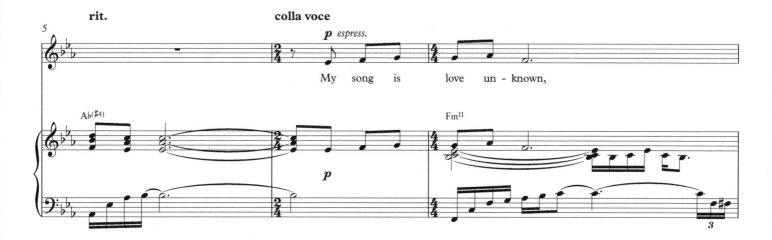

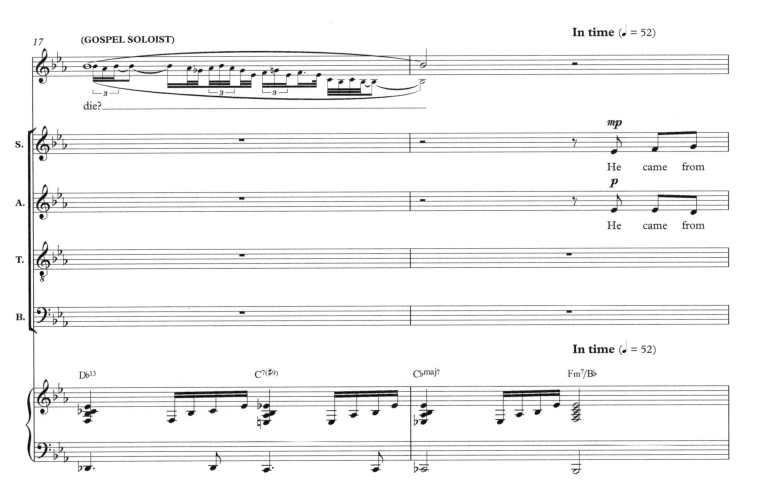

40

42

death they thirst and cry.

death they thirst and cry.

death they thirst and cry.

death they thirst and cry.

death they thirst and cry.

GOSPEL SOLOIST

Why, what hath my Lord done?

44

to inspirational mothers Mary, Jean, and Iris

5. *Stabat Mater*

13th-cent. Latin hymn

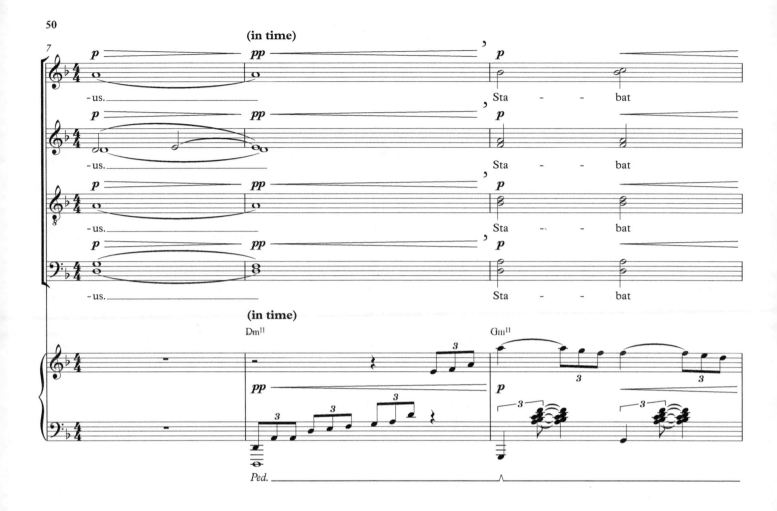

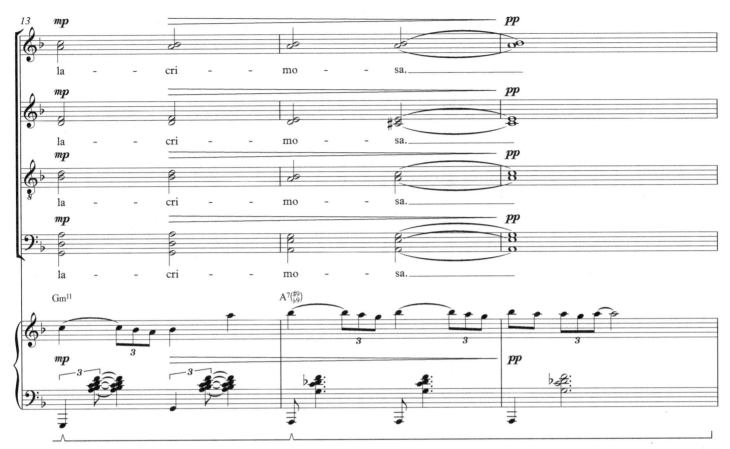

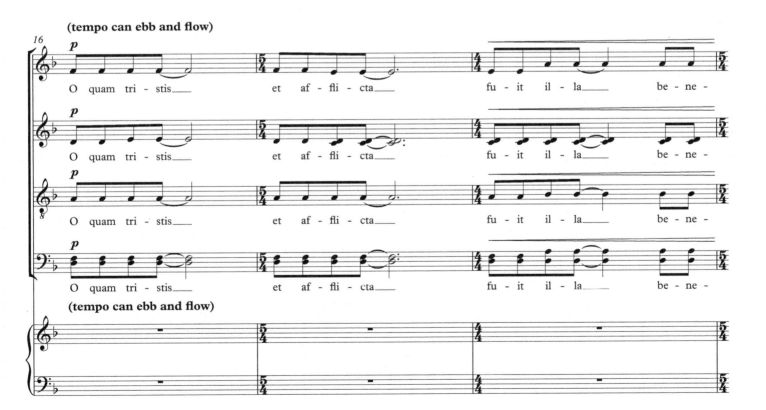

52

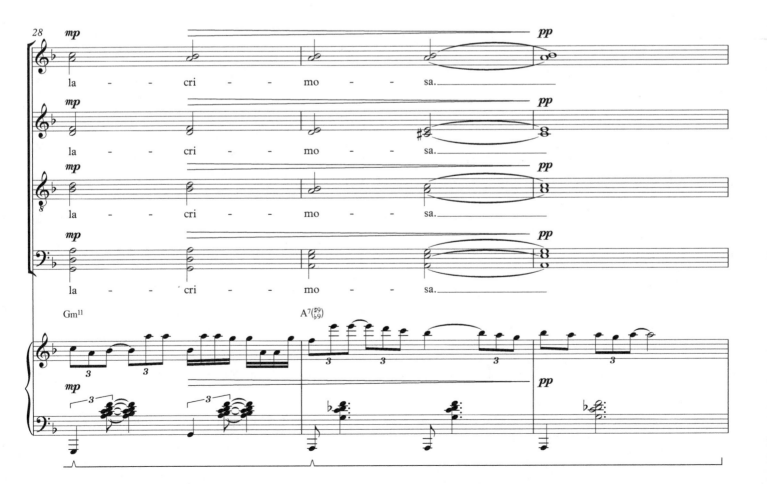

56

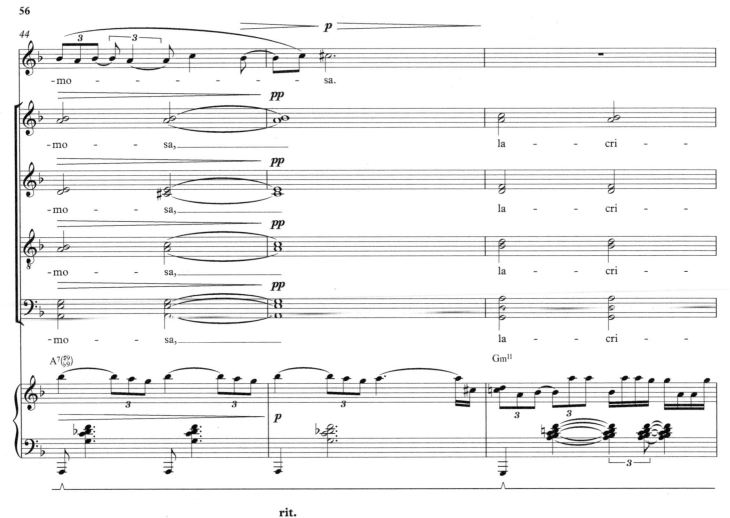

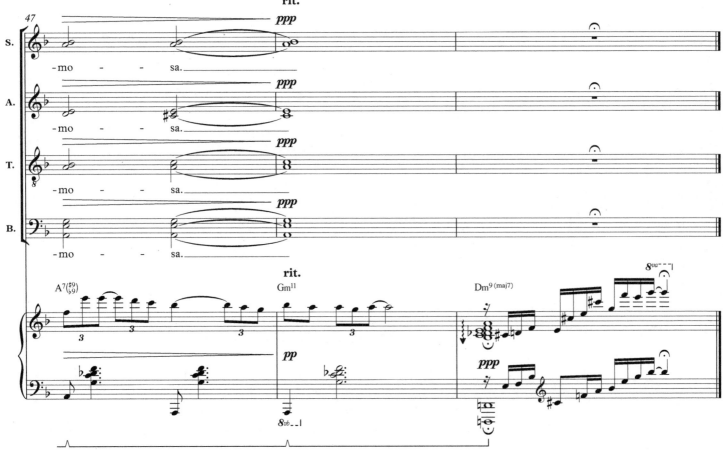

6. *The Seven Last Words from the Cross*

Will Todd, quoting The Holy Bible

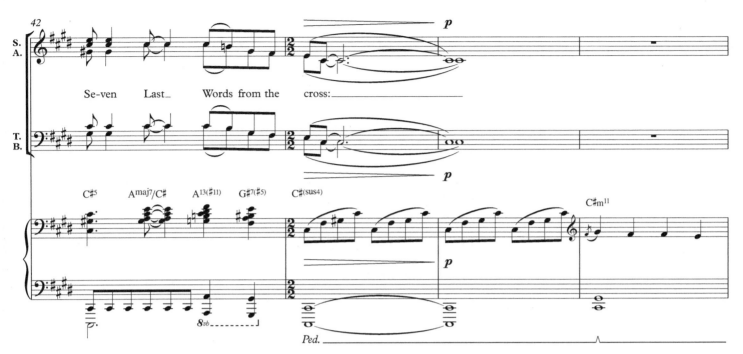

36
Se-ven Last_ Words, Se-ven Last_ Words from the
unis.
Se-ven Last_ Words, Se-ven Last_ Words, Se-ven Last_ Words from the
C♯5 Amaj7/C♯ Gmaj7/C♯ G♯7(♯5)
ff
39
cross,_ Se-ven Last_ Words._
cross,_ Se-ven Last_ Words,_ Se-ven Last_ Words,_
C♯5 Amaj7/C♯ A13(♯11) G♯7(♯5)
8vb

Se-ven Last Words from the cross:

SOPRANOS & ALTOS *unis.*

'Fa - ther, for - give____ them,_____ for they know not what they

do._____

62

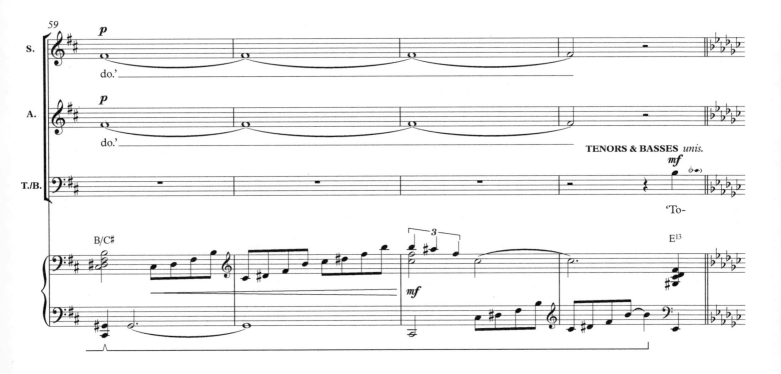

64

66

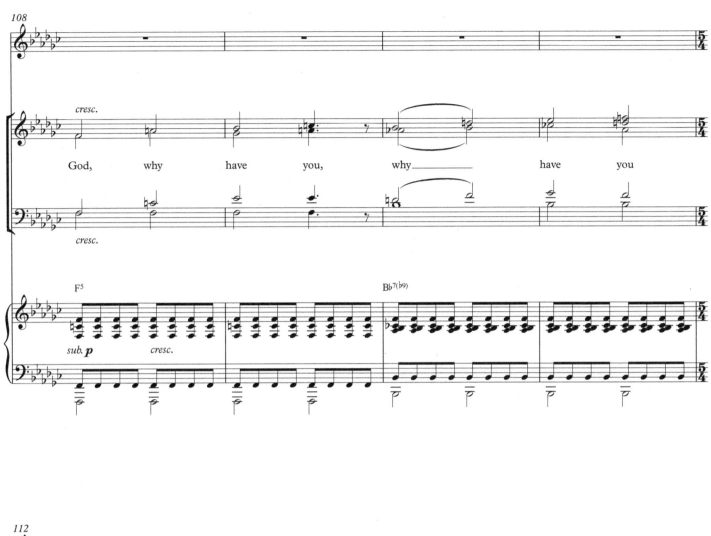

68

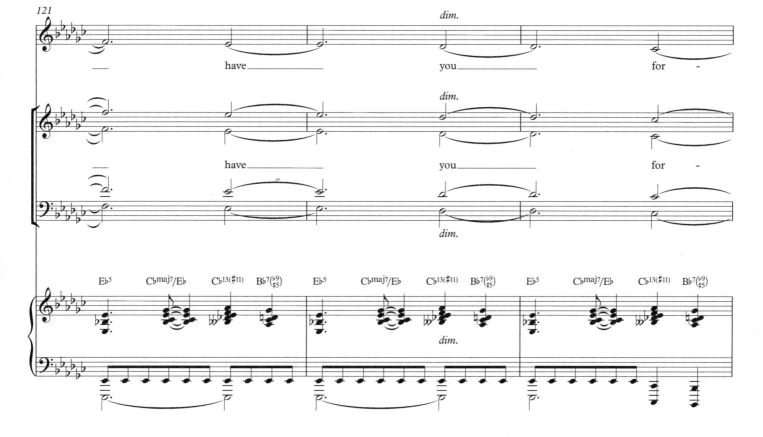

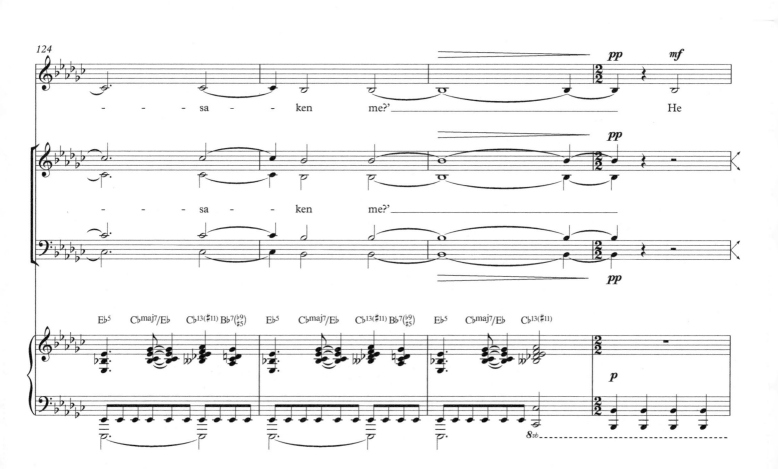

70

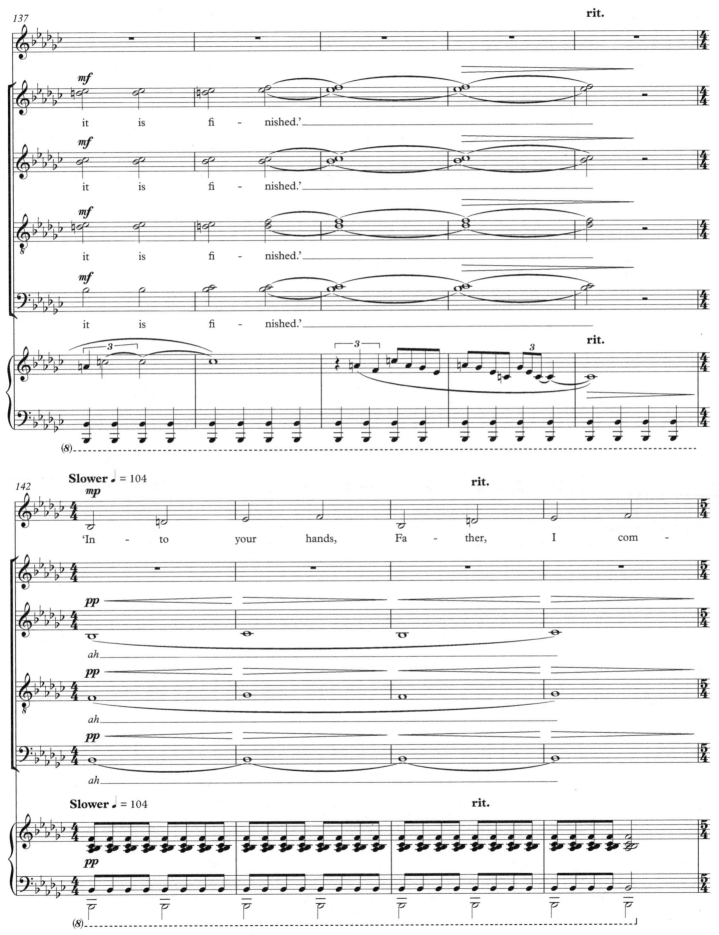

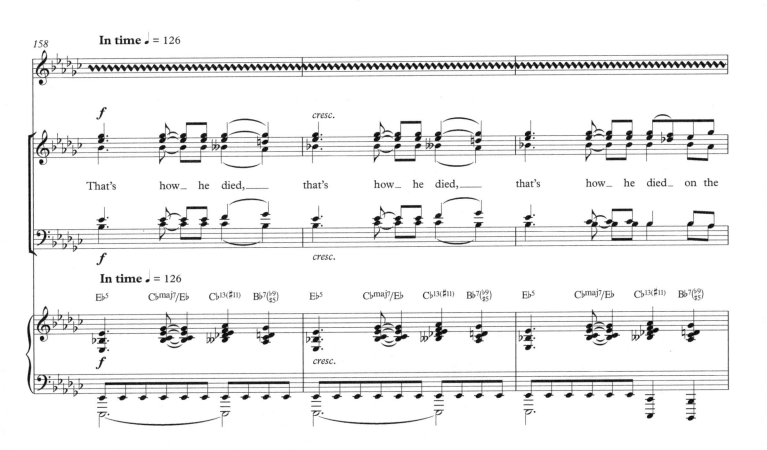

74

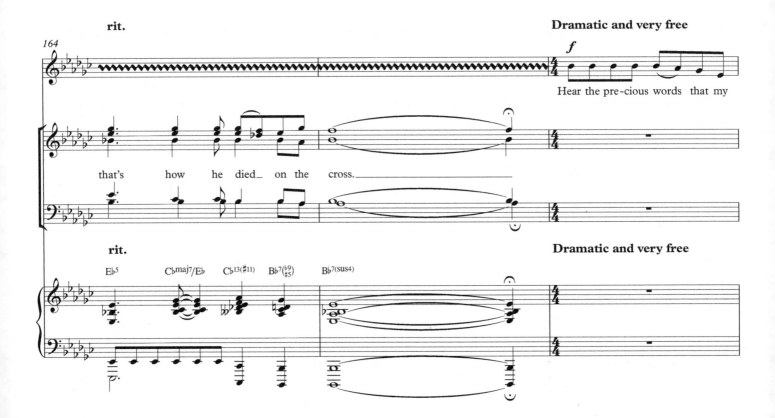

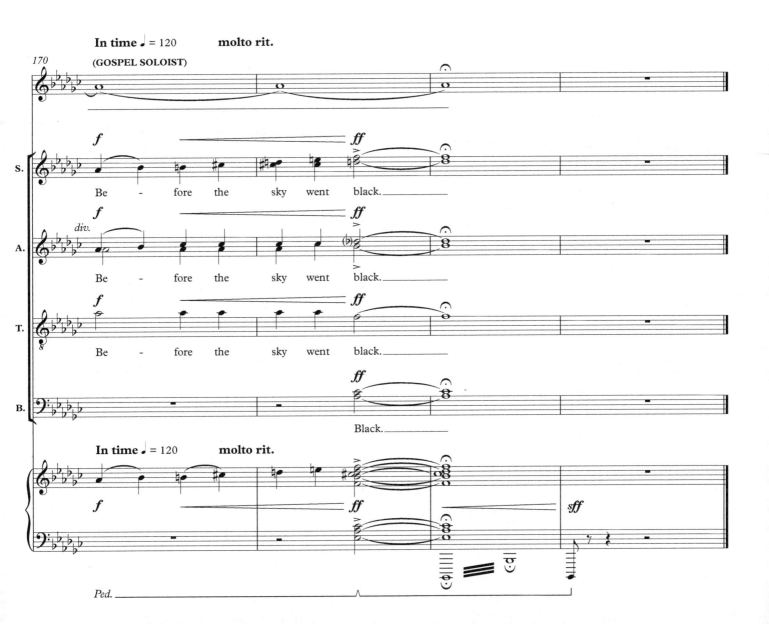

7. *My Love has Died for Me*

Will Todd

gone a-way and I have no place to go, I have no place to go.

My friend is lost to me, my friend is lost to me,

78

my friend is lost to me and I have no place to go, I____ have no

____ friend is lost to me and I have no place to go,____ I have no

my friend is lost to me and I have no place to go, I have no

my friend is lost to me and I have no place to go, I have no

place to go._____ The fire that leapt so bright - ly burned in - to e -

place to go._____ The fire that leapt so bright - ly burned in - to e -

place to go._____ The fire that leapt so bright - ly____ burned_ in - to e -

place to go._____ The fire that leapt so bright - ly burned in - to e -

8. *Do not stand at my grave and weep*

Mary Elizabeth Frye (1905–2004)

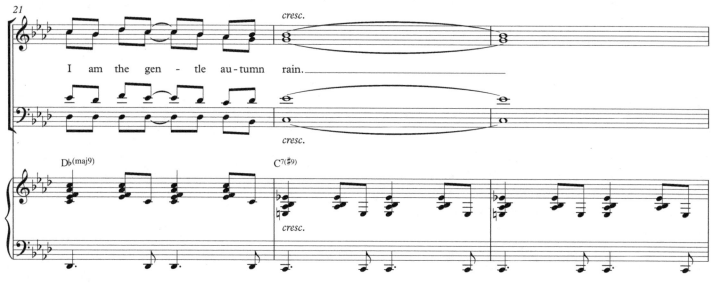

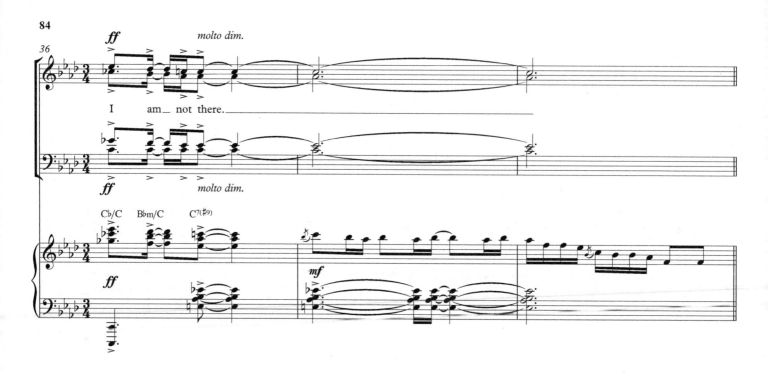

88

90

9. *Were you there?*

American Spiritual text

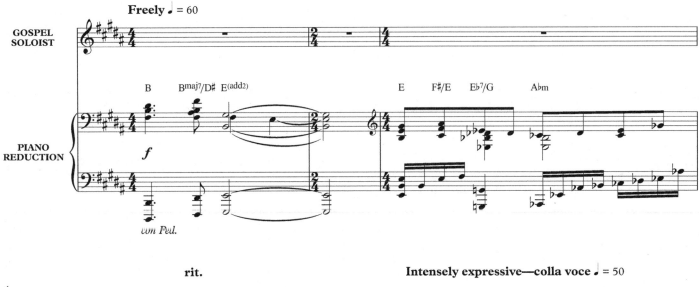

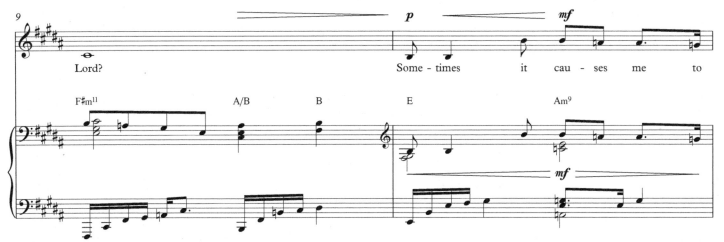

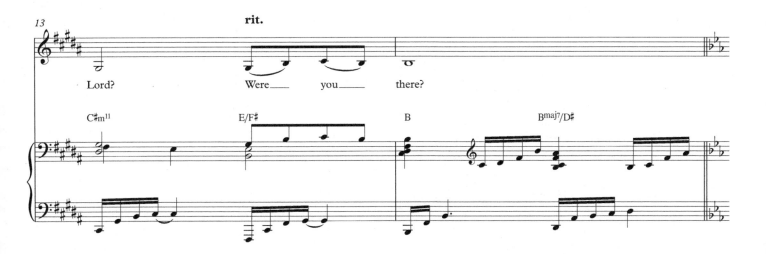

94

98

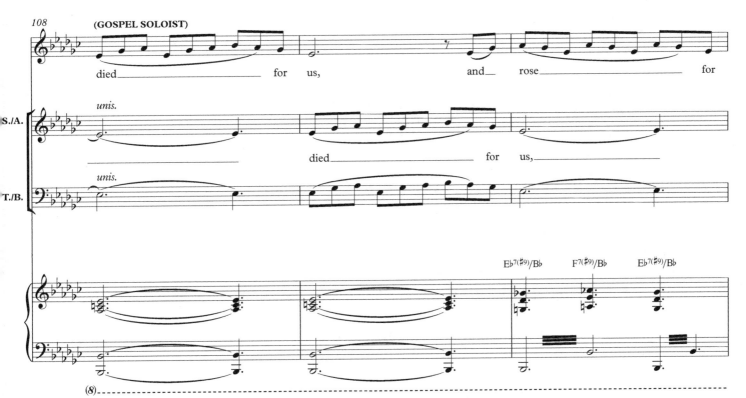

108

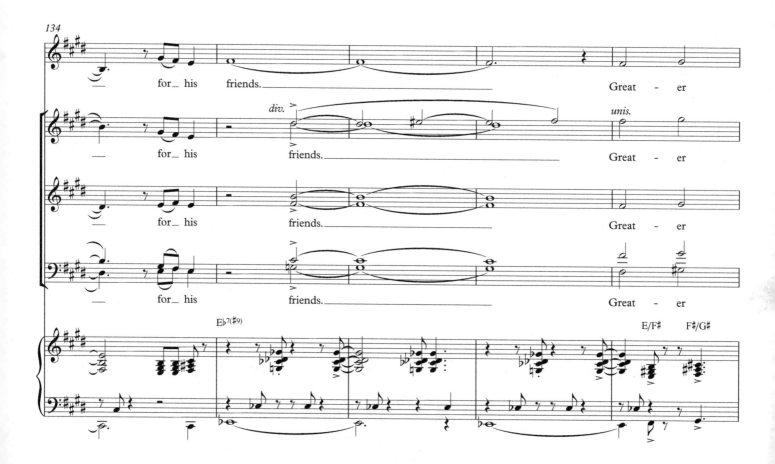

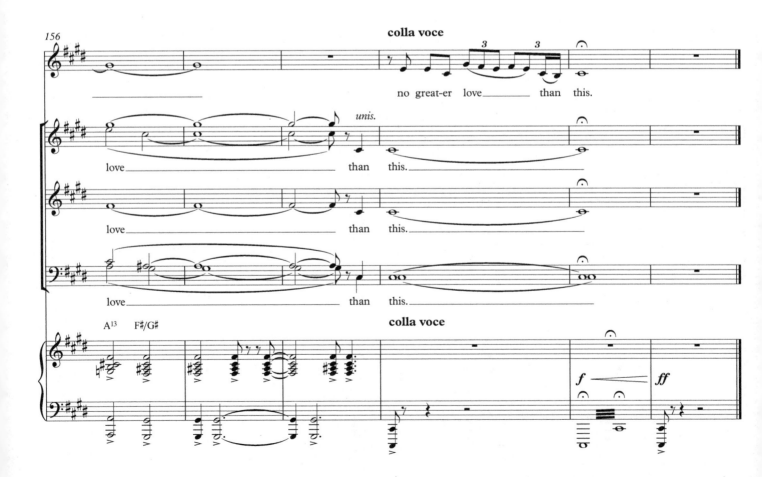